George Fisk Comfort

Modern languages in education

George Fisk Comfort

Modern languages in education

ISBN/EAN: 9783743393615

Manufactured in Europe, USA, Canada, Australia, Japa

Cover: Foto ©Paul-Georg Meister /pixelio.de

Manufactured and distributed by brebook publishing software
(www.brebook.com)

George Fisk Comfort

Modern languages in education

MODERN LANGUAGES IN EDUCATION.

In the discussion concerning the position which the study of language should occupy in a general system of education, two main views have divided, in nearly equal proportion, the educators and the patrons of education in England and America.

The advocates of one view would retain essentially the traditional classical curriculum, introducing into it, however, such changes as are demanded by the present advancement in philological science, and increasing the amount that must be read as a condition for entrance to college and for graduation. They hold that all who intend entering upon a professional life, or who aspire to a liberal education, should go through this modified and improved classical curriculum, as a necessary preliminary course of training.

The advocates of the other view, including in their ranks the great body of business men,—of those who arrogate to themselves the title of "practical men,"— hold that the ancient languages should be abolished entirely from our general system of education, and should be replaced by the modern languages and the natural sciences; or that, if studied at all, the ancient languages should be left to that small class of "useless, impractical men which infest every community, who prefer to alienate themselves from the living present and to live among the musty remains of past ages."

In many of our colleges a convenient solution of the question is sought by avoiding the issue, and admitting two parallel courses of study embodying these conflict. ing views, to which are given .the conventional names of "classical" and "scientific" courses. The "scientific" course is frequently made but three years in length, and the requirements for admission to it are usually inferior to those to the "classical" course. In a few of the best colleges another solution of the problem is sought, by retaining the old classical course and adding recitation in one or more of the modern languages during a portion of the college curriculum.

We shall endeavor to show, as well as the limits of this paper will permit, that all of the above views and methods are fundamentally wrong, and that the true solution of the question as to the position which the study. of language should occupy in our educational system is to be found in a method which is radically different from any of those at present in vogue.

By the system which we shall propose, many advantages will be gained which are unattainable under either of the present methods. A unity will be maintained in the entire academic and collegiate courses, making them the most profitable for the several classes of students: for those who, after finishing the academic course, shall enter upon the duties of active life; for those who shall continue through the college course before entering upon their careers in business or professional life; for those who shall complete the college course, as preparatory to special study in any of the learned professions; and, finally, for those who intend to become professional linguists. Thus the so-called "practical" men and the scholastic party will be reconciled and will work in harmony, instead of injuring our educational system, as they are now doing, by their distracted counsels and conflicting efforts.

To illustrate this reorganization of the linguistic part of our educational system, we will imagine one of our great cities or States having a complete system of graded schools, the whole being crowned with a post-collegiate university. The great need of such universities in America is now becoming so extensively felt that it is only a question of time as to how soon they shall be established. In all probability the next ten years will witness the founding of one or more such universities, which will soon rival, in the extent and excellence of their appointments, the largest and best universities in continental Europe. It is to be hoped that, in their plan of organization, they will be in advance of even the great and time-honored European universities, all of which retain more or less of mediæval tradition, both in their plan and their spirit. But the modification in linguistic instruction which we shall propose will greatly improve our educational system, even without these much needed post-collegiate universities.*

---

* Since the above was written (in 1872) the John Hopkins University, at Baltimore, has been established, with a number of incomplete post-graduate departments. Several times the amount of the endowment of that institution will, however, be needed to found and equip in America a university which shall be the peer of the great universities of Continental Europe. Buildings, libraries, museums, apparatus, and other appointments representing several millions of dollars, and an annual income of at least one million dollars will be requisite in order to found and sustain what we may at present term a "post-collegiate university," in which shall be given the most advanced instruction of the present age in every branch of thought and in every department of professional study. At least one hundred thousand dollars annually will be needed, in order to

According to the plan which we propose, the study of one living language will be commenced by pupils when between the ages of ten and twelve years. The method of instruction should at first be very simple, and adapted to the stage of development of the young child. As at this age the memory is more active than the judgment, and the mind inclines to details rather than to principles, the attention should be directed at this time to learning the names of the most familiar objects, and to gathering a store of familiar phrases and expressions, referring to the simplest physical facts and phenomena, and to the simplest operations and emotions of mind and heart. A body of linguistic material will thus be accumulated in this new language, as had previously been the case with the pupil's own vernacular, to be subjected in his more mature years to rigid grammatical analysis and philological treatment. The pupil should also immediately utilize what he has learned, and should be taught to express his childish thoughts, desires, and emotions in this new living language. He should also read juvenile literature in this language, of no higher grade than that which he is reading in his own vernacular. More rigid grammatical instruction will be added as soon and as fast as the intellectual development of the pupil will admit.

As much time, or more, should be given to the study of this living language in the academy or preparatory

---

sustain the philological faculty, which should contain not less than twenty professors, with salaries of not less than five thousand dollars each. The rincely and hitherto unexampled donation of twenty millions of dollars by Senator Stanford for a university in California approximates the sum needed to found, equip, and endow a great "post-collegiate" university in America.

school as is now given in them to the study of Latin. Upon entering college the student will be able to read common prose in this new language with considerable fluency, to converse with tolerable freedom upon ordinary topics, and to understand a simple discourse.

Two years before the close of the academic course, the study of a second living language should be commenced. As this will be begun when the student is at a more mature age, and as the student will have had an experience of some years in the study of language, a less slow, elementary, and juvenile method will be necessary at the outset, and the advancement will be more rapid. Indeed, upon entering college the proficiency of the student in these two languages will be nearly equal.

These two living languages will thus take the place of Latin and Greek in the studies which are required for admission to college. During the Freshman year the classical literature of these languages will be read, and the rigid philological study of them will be taken up. During the remainder of the college course, one study at a time, in other branches of science, will be pursued from text-books in one or the other of these languages. During the senior year the history of these languages, their relation to cognate languages, and the history of their literature will be introduced as elective studies.

The study of Latin will be commenced at the beginning of the Sophomore, that of Greek at the beginning of the Junior year. Each will be studied one year or more according to the choice of the individual student. During one term will be pursued the formal study of the system of derivation from Latin and Greek of words in ordinary discourse, and of technical terms in the English language.* The modifications in form and signification which words of Latin and Greek origin have received, while passing through other modern languages before they came into the English, will be pointed out, thus showing the plexus of connections that binds together the European languages. The mutual relations of the Latin and the Greek languages, and their relations to the other Indo-European languages will also be pointed out.

It will then remain for philological faculties in (post-collegiate) universities, to give that high linguistic instruction, both in the ancient and modern languages, which is so lacking in America. Associations of linguists, like the American Oriental Society, the American

---

* To illustrate, or to test how well-founded is the claim that the prolonged study of Latin and Greek (as now conducted, and without special and formal attentien being devoted this subject,) gives to the scholar ready and reliable knowledge of the etymology and the meaning of popular words and technical terms in the English that are derived from these languages, it may be interesting for any person who has graduated in the classical course in an American college to attempt to write off the etymology and the meaning of such words as the following, without having recourse to a dictionary or cyclopedia: alms, apology, apologue, apothem, aposteme, apozem, cavalry, chain, chair, chaise, cheese, cherry, chestnut, conscience, frail (adj.), frail (noun), fraise, frieze, frigate, miniature, poison, reason, season, soldier, sole (of the foot), sole (a fish), joist, journey, vouch, voyage, geography, biography, photography, typography, orthography, orthographic projection, linear perspective, integral calculus, renal calculus, geology, philology, philotaerus, euphony, euphodite, eupion, eurite, hyperbola, hypertrophy, hyperplasia, hypersthene, hydrogen, hydrastis, hydrocele, hydatid, caloric, lauric, bihenic, ether, ethyl, octyl, decatyl, butyl, museum, atheneum, delirium, palladium, ruthenium, didydium, albumen, albumenuria, albugo, myrmidon, myrmeleon, myroptera, myopia, myothera. One single term given to the formal study of etymology under a skilfull professor, at the time of the college course indicated above, will be of more value in this regard to the scientific and general student than many years devoted to the reading of the literature.

Philological Association and the recently established Modern Language Association, have also a work to perform in the promotion of philological science, which is beyond the province and beyond the power of any school of instruction. Germany has attained its high position as the home of modern philology by means of its post-collegiate universities and of its many local and specific, as well as national and general philological societies. It is only by these same instrumentalities that philology can attain, in America, a position coordinate with that which it ocupies in Germany, or even to that which medicine, law, theology, and the natural sciences occupy in this country.

Having thus sketched the outlines of this system of linguistic instruction, we shall glance rapidly at the most prominent arguments in its defense.

Language is the medium of communicating to others our thoughts, feelings, and desires through spoken words. It is of the highest importance that the young pupil should apprehend this nature and office of language at the very commencement of his studies. To the degree in which the first new language which he begins to learn, aside from his own vernacular, can be shown to him to be capable of performing this mission,—to the degree in which he can be made to see that all his thoughts, emotions, and desires, which he expresses fully and completely in English, can be disrobed of their English dress, and can be enrobed in the garb of another language,— to that degree will he apprehend the nature and office of the new language; and, in return, to that degree will his studies in the new language aid him in understanding the nature and office of his own vernacular, and finally, of language in general.

This condition can be met, in the highest degree, only in the study of a living language, and of one which is the expression of a civilization that is not very different from our own, and of a grade not lower than our own. By no means can it be fully met in studying a language which has ceased to be spoken, and which, when spoken, was the expression of a civilization that was essentially different from our own, and in many respects inferior to our own. The difficulty with reference to the ancient languages, as the basis of a system of linguistic education is also greatly aggravated by the fact that there exists in those languages none of that charming juvenile literature which is so luxuriant in the classical living languages, and which alone is adapted to the mental development of young students. Of necessity students who begin with Latin and Greek, are compelled to read the works of ancient classical literature, as the great epics of Virgil and Homer, at an age when no person would think them fitted for the study of the corresponding classical works in modern literature, as Dante's *Divina Commedia*, Racine's *Phèdre*, or Schiller's *Wallenstein*, —much less of the *Niebelungenlied*, the *Cid*, or the *Chanson de Roland*.

In order to impress most effectually upon the mind of the young student a clear idea of the nature and office of language, and of the difference between his vernacular and other languages, it is important that he should continue the study of the single language with which he commences, until he realizes that everything that he says in English can also be said in this other language. With this thought fully fixed in his mind, and fully realized in his practice, each new language that is afterwards commenced will be acquired with increasing facility and in shorter time.

It is of course far better that, when possible, the new language should be learned in the country where it is the vernacular. The learner is there surrounded by the atmosphere of the language, and takes it in at every breath. He absorbs it unconsciously as well as consciously. But this is within the reach of so few, that the real question is, how can the benefits of foreign residence be approximately realized in our schools? This must depend upon the kind of text-books employed, the method of instruction adopted, and the skill and ingenuity of the teacher; much can be done, however, to remove the artificiality of learning a language away from the country where it is the vernacular.*

Phonetics form one of the most vital elements in language. Language comes from the tongue of the speaker, and goes to the ears of the hearer. Sight should play but a very subsidiary part in the study of language. Yet sight is relied upon almost entirely in learning the ancient languages. The ordinary college student would

---

* The so-called "natural method" of learning languages, which has been recently introduced into many summer schools and into some established institutions, is a natural rebound from the unnatural grammatical method of commencing the study of languages. In many instances the results of the "natural method" in the hands of a skillful teacher and with willing pupils, have been marvellous. But it is an unpardonable error to go to the other extreme and omit entirely the study of grammar. Of necessity the grammatical, historical, philological, and philosophical methods must be introduced in due time and in right proportions, in order to secure a thorough and critical knowledge of a language. The practice should precede the principles, but should not exclude them.

be perfectly bewildered upon hearing a new sentence in Latin or Greek pronounced. He must *see* it, in order to comprehend it. But the phonetic structure of Latin and Greek is very imperfectly understood; a greater obscurity still rests upon the history of the phonetic development of those languages. To make the matter worse for the student, a perfect chaos prevails in our pronunciation of Latin and Greek. After having learned to pronounce these languages by one confessedly arbitrary system, upon going to another school, or upon entering college, he is often compelled to adopt another and very different, though equally arbitrary system of pronunciation. Truly is not this the play of Hamlet, with Hamlet left out ?—or with the part of Richard the Third, or of Falstaff, substituted for that of Hamlet? What an accurate idea the Chinese would have of the phonetic character of the English, French, and German languages, if, from their aversion to foreigners, they should refuse to admit English, French, and German teachers, and then should give their own pronunciation to all of these three languages!—or, if different Chinese teachers should adopt different methods of pronouncing these languages!

From the nature of the case, the study of phonetics can be applied, to any important extent, only to living languages. The exact pronunciation of French as spoken in Paris, of German as spoken in Berlin, and of Italian as spoken in Florence and Rome, can be perfectly ascertained and perfectly taught. Good instructors in the modern languages very properly take great pains to secure from their pupils at the outset a correct, easy and elegant pronunciation. They meet with the greatest difficulty in students who begin the study of the modern languages during the junior or senior year of the college course. The organs of speech of these advanced students are rigid and unpliable. Their ears are also slow to detect the nice distinction of elegant, or even correct pronunciation. Not unfrequently their pride is touched at their ludicrous mistakes. And, what is worse still, having been taught to consider a knowledge of grammatical forms and skill in translating to be all that is essential in studying languages, they soon look upon pronunciation as a matter of secondary importance, and worthy of the attention of only young children. These advanced college students soon become restless if a good pronunciation is insisted upon. The professor generally finds himself forced to yield, though under mental protest, and to permit his class to rush on to reading the works of Schiller, Goethe, Racine, Molière, Dante, and Tasso, though their pronunciation is yet so execrable, that it would almost make these classic writers wish to appear in the flesh, that they might seize the books from the hands of the students and cry out to them to stop murdering their productions. If the same American college student should visit a German gymnasium or a French lycée, and there hear Milton's Paradise Lost, Shakespeare's tragedies, or Longfellow's poems read with as execrable a pronunciation as is usually heard of French and German in American colleges, they would call the study of English in these schools a farce. The difficulty is inherent in our system; it is impossible to acquire a good pronunciation of French and German, when only two or three hours a week is given for some months to the study of either of these languages, especially when most of the time is devoted to the study of grammatical construction and of classic literature.

Only after the student has had long training in the study of one or more living languages, is he even partially prepared to imagine the phonetic structure of languages, the pronunciation of which has been lost.

The study of phonetics is a most valuable means of mental discipline. It also opens up one of the most important fields of psychological and physiological research. It treats of one of the chief means by which the body is made the interpreter of the spirit. It lies at the foundation of the entire science of language. It furnishes the only key to the vocal changes that take place in the history of a language, and to the vocal variations among related languages. In learning to produce those sounds in other languages which do not occur in his own vernacular, the student will acquire a new and wider view of the resources of his own vocal organs; he will be struck with the fact that some of the most frequently recurring sounds in his own language do not occur in other languages; and the whole study of phonetics, as applied to foreign languages, will induce in the student a more exact and elegant enunciation of his own language.

After the rudiments of pronunciation have been mastered, the most rapid and correct habits of analysis and synthesis are called into action in the practical use of a spoken language. The difference between the rapidity and precision of mental action which are necessary in order to understand a spoken sentence, and those which are required in order to pick out deliberately, when seated at one's desk, with grammar and dictionary at hand, the meaning of the same sentence from the printed page, is not unlike the difference in skill which is neces. sary for a sportsman to hit a bird on the wing, from that which is requisite in order to hit a painted bird in a shooting-gallery. There is an equally great difference between the rapidity and precision of mental action which are required in order to formulate a sentence in rapid conversation, and those which are necessary in order to be able to write out deliberately, when seated at a desk, with grammar and dictionary at hand, a sentence in Latin or Greek composition.

Thus, in order to understand a spoken sentence, in the first place, the hearer must rapidly and almost unconsciously separate the succession of sounds in a sentence into individual words; for, in all spoken languages, there is little if any more separation of sound recognizable to the ear between the words of a sentence, than between the syllables of a word. This difficulty is greatly increased in those languages where the final consonant is often carried over and pronounced with the following word. After having recognized the separate words in the spoken sentence, the hearer must recognize the stems of the words and the influence of terminations, prefixes and suffixes, and the influence of syntactical laws. He must also consider whether the words are employed in their primary or with derived significations, and whether the sentence contains idiomatic expressions, ellipses and other figures of speech. And, finally, he must consider the relation of the sentence to preceding conversation. All this must be done in a flash, like the taking of instantaneous photographs. Indeed, the rapid and complicated mental operations and exertions of even the young pupil, in order to understand very simple spoken sentences at their first enunciation, are none the less real and strength-giving, from the fact that they are often voluntary and unconscious, or that the ferule, the demerit-mark, and the prize are not required in order to call them forth. The number and quickness of mental operations are correspondingly greater in a more mature person, while conducting a rapid and free conversation, or while hearing a spoken discourse. The study of the dead languages offers nothing analogous for the development of rapid and almost instantaneous analytic habits and power of mind.

And, on the other hand, a person is required not only to apprehend sound rapidly and correctly by his ear; he must also produce sounds with equal rapidity and precision with his own mouth. He must give to words the proper accent, emphasis, and intonation. He must give their proper inflections, and locate and connect them in sentences according to the syntactical laws of the particular language. He must decide whether to use words in literal or in figurative significations, and when to employ idiomatic constructions and ellipses, inversions, and other figures of speech. The mind must perform the double work of directing the pronunciation, and of formulating the sentences rapidly and correctly. To converse with freedom and elegance in a foreign language presupposes long and continued practice and training, which have been as real, if not as obvious and demonstrative, as with a pianist who has learned to perform difficult music at sight. The synthetic powers of the mind are brought into action in a manner and to an extent not even approximated in the study of Latin and Greek, as generally pursued in American colleges.

While a language continues to be spoken, it cannot remain stationary, but it must be subject to growth, development, and modification, or to change or decay. Those languages whose history can be most completely traced, are necessarily the most valuable for showing the nature of linguistic growth and change. In this respect, no ancient or modern classical languages are superior to the German or the French. We can trace the growth of the German language through nearly two thousand years, from the primitive stages as the rude language of a collection of barbarous tribes, through three distinct and well-marked periods, with several subordinate divisions to each period. The French language has a well-known history, extending through more than ten centuries, with two prominent and several subordinate periods. These two languages are also yet endowed with the vital elements of growth. New words are being formed from within or added from without. Many unsettled questions concerning various linguistic features and elements in these languages are now under discussion, and will be settled in due time, as similar questions in past periods of the language have been settled. The French and German languages thus offer, within themselves, vastly more material for the illustration of the development of linguistic features, of vocal changes, grammatical forms, verbal derivation and composition, syntactical construction, the absorption of foreign elements and the effects of foreign influences, than do the Latin and Greek languages.

It would require but little reflection to lead us to anticipate, what every teacher who has given the subject a fair trial has observed, that a far greater interest is awakened in the mind of the young student by the study of a living than of a dead language. He recognizes that it can serve to him all the purposes of a language. He appropriates it and incorporates it as a part of his own mental furniture. He also utilizes it immediately, for the expression of his own thoughts, feelings, and desires, and thus is led early to form a most valuable habit— that of applying to his own individual use what he has learned theoretically. The value of this enthusiasm as a stimulus to study can hardly be over-estimated. This interest will not be confined to the years of childhood. It will be sustained through all of the academic and collegiate courses, inasmuch as the student continues to realize that other languages than the English can be the vehicle of all the thoughts and feelings of his maturing and expanding mind and heart. Various means may be employed to sustain this interest. Thus, selections in prose and poetry in these languages may be committed to memory for declamation; French and German periodicals may be introduced into the college reading-rooms, and may be occasionally used in the class-room instead of the text-book; French and German books upon history, biography, travels, the sciences and arts, and in belles-lettres literature, can be introduced into the libraries; during the latter part of the college course text-books written in these modern languages may be employed for the study of the various sciences; resident French and German men of science and letters can deliver to the senior class lectures upon French and German history and literature, and upon various branches of science. All this will serve the double purpose of giving information and entertainment to the student, and of keeping his knowledge of those languages fresh and ever advancing. These living languages, when thus acquired, will remain an unfailing and direct source of profit and pleasure during the subsequent period of study in professional schools, and during all after life. They will not pass from memory within a few years after the close of the college course, as is often the case with Latin and Greek.

As to which two modern languages should be made the basis of linguistic education in English-speaking countries, the choice would undoubtedly be given to the French and the German. Besides the reasons which would have weight in England, in determining the precedence in order of time in the study of these two languages, there is a very important one, which applies with peculiar force to our own country. America is fast losing the character of being a unilingual country. Already one-tenth of our population speak a foreign tongue. Should existing causes continue to act, before another generation shall pass away one-fifth of our entire population will be German-speaking people. German immigrants are already to be found in every village and city, and in most rural districts. American children hear the German language spoken in the streets, often by German servants in their homes, or by German schoolmates in their schools; they see German names and words on signs of stores and hotels; they hear German newspapers cried in the streets; they see German books and engravings upon the center-table. All of this gives unconscious but real education; it impresses upon the mind of the American child the fact of the real, living character of the German language; and it prepares him, even before he enters school, to commence with the study of this, rather than of the French language. Many arguments may be advanced, however, for beginning with the French rather than with the German.

By commencing with living languages and studying them in the method and at the time above proposed, the student will enter the sophomore or junior year of the college course with a much clearer view of the nature and office of language, and with much greater ability to master a new language and to understand its peculiar structure and spirit than is possible under the present system of beginning with the ancient classical languages. In a single year he could learn to read, but not to speak, Italian, Spanish, Dutch, or Swedish, as fluently as the German and French, upon which he has spent so much time. He will also have received that peculiar training which is requisite in order to study with profit a language from which the vital characteristic of being a natural and living vehicle of thought and feeling has forever gone; a language the pronunciation of which is but imperfectly known; a language which has ceased to grow, but which stands before us in the crystallized form that it assumed many centuries ago; a language which, when spoken, was the expression of a civilization that has passed away; a language of which the familiar, social, and domestic portions have perished, and of which the only remains extant are some portions of its artistic, classical literature.

With the experience and training in the study of lan-

guage which will thus be acquired, through following a
natural and logical method, and with the maturity of
mind which ordinary college students have at the beginning of the sophomore year, they will arrive at a more
correct and critical apprehension of the character, the
spirit, and the linguistic features and relations of the
Latin and Greek languages by one year of well-directed
study, if commenced at this period, than most college
students attain to, through the present method, by the
end of the college course. If, during the one or two
years which will thus be devoted to the study of each of
the ancient languages, not as many Latin and Greek
authors can be read as at present, those which shall be
read will be better understood; and a clearer view can
be gained of the general spirit of ancient literature, and
of its relation to modern literature, as well as of the linguistic relations of the ancient to the modern languages.

Such of the Latin and Greek authors, which are now
read in college, as cannot be pursued in the time that
will thus be devoted in the college course to the study
of the ancient languages, will be read more profitably
under the instruction of philological faculties in post-
collegiate universities, or in special schools of philology.
Under these philological faculties of universities, all of
the ancient and modern classical languages and literatures will be taught from the highest standpoint of
modern philology, and after a method which is adapted
to the intellectual development and linguistic attain-
ments of college graduates, who will form the chief body
of the students of such a university.

This modification of our system of linguistic instruction will produce many valuable results. In the first

place, it offers the only feasible plan for the education of professional linguists; in order to meet the present deficiency of university instruction in philology, candidates for professorships of language in our colleges, and others in America who devote themselves to special branches of philological investigation, are forced to go through tedious years of undirected private study, or to seek, as almoners, in foreign lands advantages which are denied them at home. But, aside from this most important consideration, the plan proposed above provides the best preliminary linguistic education for those who shall enter any of the learned professions; it also gives the most profitable study to that large class, including indeed the great majority of students, who, for various reasons, do not go beyond the academic course, or do not finish the collegiate course. It is no small advantage, also, that a symmetry will thus be maintained in the linguistic part of our educational system.

It is a not unimportant factor in this discussion that the modern languages present a vast amount of most varied literature, which can be properly read by young and older students, either separately or in classes, and of which expurgated editions are not needed, in order not to offend or injure the virtuous and high-minded youth of both sexes. This is especially true of classic works written during the present century, since women now form in all cultivated lands so much larger a proportion of the reading and educated public than in any former period in history.

Furthermore, it is not extravagant to state that, in every branch of human learning and investigation, fully four-fifths of the advanced knowledge and thought of the world is published in the German and the French languages. The German language holds to-day very nearly the same relation to the English that the Italian did to the German during the sixteenth and seventeenth centuries, or that the Greek did to the Latin at the time of the Roman Empire. In quantity and value of records of new and independent investigation and discovery, the French comes next to the German, though far removed from it. Then follow at about equal pace the English and the Italian. The English-speaking student or professional man who is able to read fluently the German and the French languages, has access thereby to nearly all the valuable results of investigation at the present day in any department of human knowledge. Per contra, a person who cannot read these languages fluently is thereby cut off from the great mass of the advanced thought of the world. The retrograde condition of professional scholarship in America to-day, in comparison with that in continental Europe, is owing in no small degree to the fact that so large a proportion of the graduates and even of the professors and presidents of our colleges and universities have in the past been unable to read with freedom, if at all, any other living language than their own vernacular. Only in the rarest cases, and then with the greatest difficulty, is the ability to do so acquired after a person has entered upon the active duties of his professional career.

Only a small portion of the literature which appears in any language, whether technical, artistic, or popular, and whether in the permanent form of books or in serial periodicals, is ever translated into any other language. Such translations as are made are not printed, at the earliest, until some months, more usually not until some years, after the original works have been published. "The children of this world are," indeed, "wiser in their generation than the children of light." This is as true in matters referring to education as to religion. Not even the most stupid banker or merchant in an interior city or village would be guided in his purchases and sales by quotations in prices that ruled ten, twenty, or fifty years ago. To do so would soon bring him to bankruptcy. Nor would he be satisfied with the chance information as to market prices which he might be able to pick up from the stray newspaper of the current year that may casually fall into his hands. He subscribes to such papers as are necessary in order to keep himself posted as to the latest fluctuations in prices. But, in America, the teacher of high or low degree, the scientist and the professional man, often goes on using theories, hypotheses, opinions and data which were current and deemed reliable a decade or a generation ago, not seemingly aware that they have long since been laid aside by all who keep abreast with the progress of human knowledge, and not perceiving that the meager education which which he received twenty years or more ago is very inadequate equipment for educational and professional work at the present time. By rapid communication, abundant travel, and extensive and careful study in other lands, the solidarity among nations has so greatly increased in recent times that Boston, New York, and Baltimore are much nearer to Berlin, Munich, and Paris to-day than Baltimore was to Boston fifty years ago. While the ability to read German and French freely is a valuable acquisition to the man of

business in America, as in other countries, it is an abso-
lute necessity to the educator, the investigator, and the
professional man who does not wish to be left hope-
lessly in the rear by those who have this ability and use
it. No amount of acquaintance with the Latin and
Greek languages will supply the deficiency of a knowledge of either of these modern classical languages.

It ought to be humiliating to a gentleman claiming to
be liberally educated, especially if he occupies a position of professional prominence, to find himself unable
to pronounce correctly the names of sovereigns, states-
men, scientists, artists, and men of letters in the leading
nations of Europe, or to find himself unable to understand such simple quotations or apothegms in these languages as are current in society and literature, and, by
such mispronunciation or ignorance, to find himself
laughed at by school-misses in their teens. The past
may bury the past. But the educated gentleman and
professional scholar of the coming generation cannot af-
ford to have his scholarship discounted at home and
abroad by even this superficial test.

In discussing the value of different kinds of study in
a system of education, consideration should be given not
only to the value of the discipline given and of the information actually acquired through the subjects pursued, but also, and a very important degree, to the
extent in which the knowledge thereby attained can be
made use of in the practical work of life, whether in
business or in the professions.* As we have shown

* In confirmation of this, we add the following paragraph from a recent Circular of Information issued by the Bureau of Education (No. 3,
1885, page 39) taken from the Report of the British Commissioners upon
the state of Manufactures on the continent of Europe:

above, the modern languages meet all these conditions,
especially the last, in a very high degree.

After having stated thus briefly some of the advantages which will be gained by the proposed system, we
will consider some of the most prominent objections
which will be offered against it.

The objection has been urged [since this paper was
first published, in 1872] that there is not a sufficient supply of teachers of modern languages possessing the ade-
quate pedagogical and scholastic training to carry out
effectively the above plan in all the secondary schools
and in all the colleges and universities of our country.
Unfortunately it is too true that in times past great
discredit has been brought upon the modern languages
in our colleges by this department having often been
given, as a tentative experiment, into the hands of inex-
perienced foreigners, who were accidents or adventurers
in their profession and could not fail to bring discredit
upon any department in which they might, as accidents
or adventurers, be called to teach. Undoubtedly it is
also a great advantage to the classicists, in this, as in
other similar controversies, that there is in our country a
great abundance of competent teachers of Latin and
Greek for schools of every grade. If the reform above
described shall ever take place, or whenever and in

"Your commissioners cannot repeat too often that they have been im-
pressed with the general intelligence and technical knowledge of the
masters and managers of industrial establishments on the continent.

"They have found that these persons, as a rule, possess a sound knowledge of the sciences upon which their industry depends.

"They are familiar with every new scientific discovery of importance,
and appreciate its applicability to their special industry. They adopt not
only the inventions and improvements made in their own country, but
also those of the world at large, thanks to their knowledge of foreign
languages and of the conditions of manufacture prevalent elsewhere."

whatever degree it shall take place, it will be effected gradually, and the law of demand and supply may be trusted to prevail in this as in all other cases. It is safe to say that, at the present time, the supply of competent instructors in the modern languages for either colleges or secondary schools is considerably in excess of the demand. Many professors and teachers in this department feel keenly that the limited time usually allotted to this subject in the curriculums of study does not. permit them to accomplish any very important results.

Returning to the theoretical discussion,—it is argued that we should commence with the study of the ancient languages because the modern are derived from the ancient. Whatever force there may be in this argument with reference to French as derived from Latin, it has no bearing upon German and Greek, both of which are yet to be considered as primitive languages, or rather as sister languages, derived from a common, but undiscovered, Aryan language. But the argument proves too much. It proves that we should study Gothic, Old German, and Middle German before we study New German; that we should study Old French before New French, and the older Sanscrit before the newer Latin and Greek. On the contrary, the natural order in the study of language, as of every other branch of knowledge, is to proceed from the nearer and the more similar to the more distant and the more dissimilar. The mutual relationship of the two languages will be as clearly discerned by the student, if, in studying Latin, he finds it to be the parent of French, which he has already learned, as though, in studying French, he finds it to be the daughter of the Latin, which he has already studied. And a previous knowledge of French, if acquired in the manner proposed, facilitates the learning of Latin quite as much as, or even more than a previous knowledge of Latin facilitates the learning of French.

The fact that so many English words are derived from the Latin is often urged as an argument for the early study of this language. This is a valid argument for the study of Latin, but not for beginning the study of language with Latin. Indeed a large portion of the words of Latin origin in the English language, especially of those which are most frequently used in ordinary discourse, have come through the French into the English language. The derivation and the present forms of most of these words can only be explained by reference to the French first, and to the Latin afterwards. Very little practical application of the derivation of technical terms, which have come from Latin and Greek directly into the English language, is made by the student before he enters the sophomore year.

Nor is the claim a valid one that the ancient classical are more perfect in structure than the modern classical languages. In the summation of their grammatical elements and linguistic features, French and German are fully equal to Latin and Greek. In many respects they are indeed superior. Their vocabularies are very much larger and more varied. Their stores of idiomatic expressions are inexhaustible, and are necessarily greatly superior to the idioms which are extant in Greek and Latin literature. The number of words and idioms in these, as in all living languages, is constantly increasing The phonetic character of living languages is perfectly understood. French and German offer more material and greater scope for illustrating the laws of linguistic growth and change than Latin and Greek do within themselves.

The claim is often made that the study of the ancient languages gives a better mental discipline than can be derived from any other study. That better mental discipline is obtained from pursuing a long and systematic course of study of any kind, than by following a short, rambling, and fragmentary course, should be no matter of surprise. To say that a person has graduated in the so-called "classical" course is equivalent to saying, not only that he has studied Latin and Greek systematically and rigidly for six or eight years, but also that he has studied mathematics equally long, and that he has given the equivalent of two or three years of time to the study of other branches of science. It would indeed be a matter of great surprise if this course of study, extending thus through eight or more successive years, taking the student when his mind is most plastic and retaining him till the character is mature and fixed, even if it be not the very best that could be devised, should not give better mental discipline than do the shorter and less systematic courses of study which are generally pursued by those who do not complete the classical curriculum. It is unfair, however, to credit all the mental discipline that is gained by those who follow the classical course to the study of Latin and Greek; a fair share of this discipline should be credited to mathematics, and to the other studies that are pursued with equal vigor with the ancient languages.

In comparing the intellectual benefits to be derived from the study of the ancient and of the modern languages, we must not omit to take into account the interest that is awakened in the mind of the young pupil by the study of the latter, which interest is continued unabated through the whole course of study, and which remains active during the entire subsequent life, after leaving the academy, college, or professional school. It is not necessary for us to examine whether any portion of the mental discipline which is derived from the study of the ancient languages comes through the young pupil or even the maturer student forcing himself to a distasteful task, of which he does not realize the significance or the importance; nor whether any of the distaste to the study of Latin and Greek which may now exist, would be diminished or removed by transferring these languages to the middle or latter half of the college curriculum.

Very often, also, sufficient importance is not given to the natural and voluntary, if not indeed unconscious, but still none the less real and strength-giving exertions of mind; to the clear and rapid analysis and synthesis that that are called forth in learning to read, write, hear, and speak a living language; nor to the fact that what would be considered extraordinary proficiency in Latin and Greek would be called very moderate proficiency in a modern language.

When thus compared in all their relations and effects as a means of giving discipline to the mind, the preponderance is largely in favor of the modern languages.

Some classicists attempt to break the force of the argument against giving the lion's share of the time in the academic and collegiate courses of study to Latin and Greek, by asserting that these languages can be revitalized, and can be made to seem as natural to the student as his own vernacular, or as French and German; and they fortify their position by some striking illustrations. Thus, it is true that lectures were given in Latin in nearly all of the European universities from the fourteenth to the seventeenth century; most of the important works on science and philosophy that appeared in Europe even down to the eighteenth century were written in Latin; and Latin was the medium of correspondence and conversation between learned men of different nationalities during the same period. We may say that, in a modified sense, the Latin language (rather an unnatural, factitious Latin) has been a living language until the present century. In a more limited degree than formerly, it may be called a spoken language at the present day; the proceedings of the late Œcumenical Council of the Roman Catholic Church* were conducted in this modern factitious Latin; many of the officials of the Roman Catholic Church all over the world, and many of the professors in the universities, gymnasia, and lycées of Europe speak this Latin with greater or less proficiency. But it cannot be claimed that to the general student in America the practical advantages to be derived from learning to speak Latin, as a means of intercourse, are to-day at all commensurate with the time and labor it requires. Much less is there any equivalent for the time and labor, passing by the question of genius, which are requisite in order to compose poems in Latin and Greek, as is done in the English universities and some other institutions which pride

---

* Held in the Vatican in 1870.

themselves upon the perfection to which they carry the study of the ancient languages.

Lord Brougham learned French in his youth from an aged and highly cultivated French "gentleman of the olden style," who in bearing, manners, and language seemed a crystallized relic of the age of Louis XIV., and who had fled to England to escape the terrors of the First Revolution; when Lord Brougham went to Paris, some forty years afterwards, his antiquated French called forth many a smile. Several years ago, a distinguished professor of the University of Edinburgh, who had learned German by reading standard German literature, went to Berlin and there conversed in the language as he had learned it; his sentences were stately, cumbered, and formal, and often he was unintelligible; "that is not the German that we speak," remarked a Berlin professor. And no doubt if the ghosts of Cicero, Horace, and Virgil could hear three modern professors from Germany, France, and America talking Latin in Rome, Pompeii, or Tivoli, they would be much surprised to learn that these three professors were speaking in the languages in which they themselves wrote.

It is correct to apply the term factitious to all the Latin that has been spoken for the last thousand years. For, if it is impossible to learn to speak a contemporary living language from reading its classical literature, in which the expressions and idioms of familiar conversation do not occur, how much more is it impossible to learn to converse in Latin and Greek by the study of their classical literatures; most of the familiar expressions of these ancient languages are lost; and, what is more fatal, words, expressions, and idioms never existed in those languages to represent the new features, the mechanical appliances, the relations of trade, science, art, religion, government, and social life which characterizes modern times. Thus we have no means for determining whether, if the Latin language had continued to be the vernacular in Italy, the Romans would have adopted a word analogous to the Italian *stivale*, or one analagous to the French *botte*, as the name of the modern "boot," or whether they would have adopted another word altogether; we cannot tell whether they would have applied the name *gymnasium*, *lyceum*, *collegium*, or some other name to a school preparatory to the modern university; we cannot tell whether they would have used an expression similar to the French *banque succursale*, one similar to the Italian *banca filiale*, or another expression altogether to indicate a "branch bank." It is as absurd to manufacture Latin words and idioms, or to give a Latin dress to English words and idioms, as it would be to manufacture French and German words and idioms, or to give a French or German dress to English words and idioms. All such work should be left to the charlatans who invent universal languages. The use of such factitious Latin should be abandoned, as cultivating wrong habits of mind, and doing violence to all correct ideas of the nature of language, and of its method of growth.

But this part of the discussion seems almost needless in America to-day. For it is doubtful whether, if we except some of the best Roman Catholic colleges and seminaries, ten sentences of conversational Latin are pronounced in a year, within the hearing of students in all the colleges of the country put together. And probably there are not ten persons in Europe and America who can conduct for five minutes a free conversation in classical Greek. But still if Latin, even this factitious Latin, is not used as a means of intercourse by conversation and writing, Latin loses, to the young pupil, one of the chief characteristics of a real language.

The importance of Greek and Roman culture, as the parents (rather the grandparents) of modern culture, is often urged as a strong reason for giving to the Latin and Greek languages so early and so large a place in our educational system. But if, in viewing the question from the standpoint of the history of civilization, we shall be compelled to admit that so great a predominance should be given to the study of classical antiquity, that will not justify giving the attention solely to the study of ancient classical literature, which is but one element in ancient classical culture. Architecture, sculpture, and painting are as important elements in civilization as their sister art, literature. The whole framework of society is held together by law. The influence of Greek architecture, sculpture, and painting upon the formative arts in all their subsequent periods, and of Roman law upon mediæval and modern legislation, has been more extensive, direct, and intimate than has been the influence of Greek and Roman literature upon mediæval and modern literature. And yet what prominence is given in our academies and colleges, to the study of Greek and Roman art and of Roman law? Almost none at all.

It may be remarked, in passing, that classicists generally overlook the bearings of the extraordinary fact that the Greeks reached their high culture, not by studying the languages of other older and more refined nations (as the ancient Assyrians and Egyptians), but by "study-

ing when boys what they would need to practice when
men;" they studied their own history, their own government, their own literature, and art; being thus im-
bued with the spirit of their own civilization, they were
prepared to promote and advance it; they were not
imitators or copyists, but originators and inventors. If
America is to rise to a high stage of culture by the same
means by which Greece rose to its high culture, it will
also be by "studying when boys what we will need to
practice when men," which will not consist mostly in
reading Latin and Greek.

But it is not necessary, in order to understand the
civilization of a people with tolerable accuracy, for the
general student to study their language at all. Every
person of ordinary intelligence to-day has a fair idea of
the kind and degree of civilization existing in China,
Japan, Turkey, Madagascar, and the Feejee Islands,
without knowing a word of the languages of those
countries. Every child of twelve years of age in a
Christian family, is better acquainted with the history
of the ancient Jews than of his own nation, and this
without knowing a word of Hebrew. Most persons of
liberal education have as correct and intimate knowledge
of the civilization of the ancient Egyptians, and Assyrians, and Persians as of the ancient Greeks and Romans,
and this without deciphering a single hieroglyphic or
cuneiform inscription.

Humboldt's *Cosmos*, Ranke's *History of the Popes*, Mar-
tin's *History of France*, and Cousin's *Lectures on Philosophy*
are as well understood in the English translations as in
their original French and German dress. English translations of the writings of Plutarch, Pliny, Vitruvius,

Strabo, and Pausanius convey as accurate information as their Latin and Greek originals. Most classical scholars even derive nearly all of their knowledge of the philosophical writings of Plato and Aristotle from English translations. Almost the entire mass of Christians in all lands depend, of necessity, upon translations of the Holy Scriptures for information and stimulus, which they believe to affect their most vital eternal interests.

With poetry and other kinds of imaginative literature it is somewhat different. Here so much of the genius of the writer is shown in his peculiar employment of words, expressions, idioms, and figures of speech; his style is so engrafted into the vital elements of his own native language, that much of the freshness, vitality, and peculiar character of the original is necesssarily lost in translation. Still, much of the force and sublimity of the majestic poems of Job, Isaiah, and of Jeremiah, and of the beauty and pathos, and at times of the sublimity of the Psalms of David is retained in the English translation of the Holy Scriptures. Much of the poetic spirit is preserved, and all the development of the plot is presented in the English translations of Goethe's *Faust*, Auerbach's *Villa on the Rhine*, Hugo's *Les Misérables*, Dante's *Divina Commedia*, and the adventures of *Don Quixote;* the same is equally true of translations of the *Iliad* of Homer, the *Æneid* of Virgil, the *Odes* of Horace and Aristophanes, and the *Rigveda*.

It is not necessary for the general student to read Latin and Greek at all in order to gain an accurate knowledge of all the facts recorded by the ancient historians and of the views of the ancient philosophers; nor, indeed, in order to obtain a very tolerable knowl-

edge of the spirit and scope of classical literature. It is
to translations of the works of the classical writers,
which have been carefully made by critical scholars, and
to the masterly compilations of historians and archæolo-
gists like Grote, Merivale, Mommsen, Curtius, Winkel-
mann, Müller, Gerhard, and Rossi, that the great majority of even liberally educated persons are indebted for
the chief part of their knowledge of classical antiquity.

The primitive sources of civilization, however were
not in Greece or Rome. They were in Egypt and West-
ern and Central Asia. And modern history and civilization are more intimately connected with mediæval
than they are with ancient classical history and civilization.

Whatever time, therefore, in our general system of
education is given to the study of the history of civilization should be devoted symmetrically and equitably
to all the important features and to all the chief periods
of history, without giving undue prominence to any particular feature or period.

If, in the discussion concerning the position which
languages should occupy in our educational system, the
importance of the study of the ancient languages has
been unduly depreciated by the advocates of the "new
education," this has been in a great measure the conse-
quence of the exaggerated and indefensible claims that
have been brought forward by classicists in defense of
a traditional system, which was established in past ages,
under circumstances that no longer exist, and before the
rise of the many branches of natural, linguistic, and æs-
thetic science which have sprung into existence during
the present century, and which now claim a place beside

their elder, but not, therefore, more worthy sisters, in the educational systems of the present age.

To eliminate the ancient classical languages entirely from the course of study of any person who aspires to a liberal education, or who purposes to enter any of the learned professions, would be a serious error. The plan of reorganization proposed above does not require us to form an opinion as to whether it would not be a greater evil to reject the modern languages from the academic and collegiate courses, as has often been, and is yet not unfrequently done.

It seeks to give to the old and the new their appropriate places, to harmonize conflicting influences, and thus to give completeness and symmetry to the modern system of a liberal education.